at my SAVIOR'S FEET

Life-changing Lessons
FROM THE MASTER STORYTELLER

Authors

Ali Shaw • Alyssa Howard • Cheli Sigler

Kat Lee • Kelly LaFram • Lindsey Bell • Patti Brown

Hellomornings.org

AT MY SAVIOR'S FEET

TABLE OF CONTENTS

THE NEW Hellomornings BIBLE STUDY METHOD

We (The HelloMornings Team) are SO excited to share this new Bible study method with you!

The heart behind the method is "For Every Woman in Every Season." Whether you have 5 minutes or 50 minutes every morning, the HelloMornings study method can adapt to your schedule. We designed it so that a new believer won't feel overwhelmed and a seasoned Bible study student can dive deep into each passage.

We had three main goals in creating this method:

1. TO BUILD YOUR HABIT

Because building a daily God time habit is at the core of HelloMornings, we want to make sure you never feel overwhelmed with each day's study. If you only have 5 minutes, you can read the passage, write the verse and respond in a written prayer. If you have more time, you can dig deeper with one, two or all of the study "action steps." And if you want to go even deeper (or stretch the study out to a Saturday or Sunday) we are including group of study ideas in the front of the ebook so you'll always have a treasure trove of options to choose from.

2. TO BUILD YOUR GROUP

Our second goal was to create a method that encourages group interaction. Groups are integral to what we do here at HelloMornings. They are a way to build community, stay accountable to growth and learn from different perspectives.

But it's hard to find a group where everyone is at the same level of studying Scripture. That means with most Bible studies, some group members feel overwhelmed while others feel bored. Our goal is to bridge that gap and create content that not only fits any schedule, but also fits any level of study.

The beauty of this is that someone in your group who is brand new to the faith can daily dive into the same scriptures as a group leader who has been studying for decades. And the way we have formatted the content allows for each to learn and share in whatever way God is leading them so everyone can feel they have something to contribute, if they choose.

3. TO BUILD YOUR ROUTINE

In order to be the "hands and feet of Jesus," we need to:

1. Know Him - (God)
2. Understand His purpose for our lives - (Plan)
3. Follow His leading - (Move)

These are the core habits of HelloMornings.

God. Plan. Move.

Time with God is essential. And we believe that God has a purpose for each one of our lives. We also believe that He even has a purpose for each of our days. There are people He may want you to encourage today or ways He wants you to take action.

That is why we Plan. We want our daily planning to be done with His purposes in mind. Each daily worksheet has space for just a few of the most important tasks. Prayerfully planning is more powerful than any fancy productivity system because only God knows our heart, our purpose and our circumstances.

Finally, it's time to Move. This doesn't need to be a 3-mile run or a 25-minute workout. We simply want to be "fit for our calling" - i.e. have the energy to walk out the plan toward our purpose. If God has things He'd like us to do today, it's our responsibility to have the energy to do them. He does not give us more than we can handle.

For some, this might be simply drinking a morning glass of water. For others, it might be a short workout and for others it might be a healthy breakfast. The goal is just to do what we can to have the energy to respond to whatever God is calling us to each day. Kind of like an athlete makes sure to eat a good breakfast before a game so she has the energy to play well.

God. Plan. Move.

It doesn't need to take a long time. It could be as simple as a 5-minute routine of reading the daily passage, jotting down a few tasks and drinking a glass of water. Or it could be longer and more customized to your life.

Ultimately, we just want to start each day with the One who gave us all our days. And we want to plan our lives with the One who gives us our lives. And we want to Move wherever He may lead.

To a life well lived for the good of others and the glory of God,

The HelloMornings Team

SHARE THE STUDY

Will you consider helping us spread the word?

If you're in a HelloMornings group, invite all your group members to upgrade from the basic reading plan to this full study. It is well worth the price of a latte to study scripture deeply for 6 weeks and build a solid morning routine.

If you don't have a HelloMornings group, gather some friends together, send them to *HelloMornings.org/shop* to grab a copy of the study and spend the next 6 weeks journeying together! It's so much more fun and impactful when we learn and grow in community.

WAYS TO HELP OTHERS:

Use the hashtag *#HelloMornings* on Twitter or Instagram.

Share what you're learning on Facebook and link to *HelloMornings.org*

Tell your friends! Text, email or invite them to join you the next time you see them.

GET ALL THE RESOURCES:

We want to equip you to build a brilliant, God centered morning routine that leaves you feeling refueled and ready for action each day.

If you're not already on our email list, visit *HelloMornings.org* to download our free resources and receive our inspiring and idea-filled newsletter.

THE BIG BIBLE STUDY IDEA LIST

Each day of a HelloMornings study is filled with passages to read, a verse to write and plenty of action steps to take. But if you're ready to dive even deeper or you want to stretch our 5 day a week studies into 7 days, this list is the perfect way for you to add "tools" to your Bible study tool belt.

If you finish the study for the day and have more time, simply refer back to this "Big Bible Study Idea List" to select a few ways to dive even deeper into the passage you've been reading.

The best thing about this list is that it can be used on ANY section of scripture. So, if you want to do a study on 1 Corinthians 13 or look up all the verses on Faith, just use this list to build your own Bible study!

We want to equip you to study the Bible deeply regardless of whether you have a Bible study guide you're going through at the time or not. Try out each of these "tools" and add them to your Bible study "tool belt!"

READ AND WRITE

Ways to study scripture and dig deep into one passage.

READ

Simply read the passage. You can read it in your head, read out loud, read thoughtfully and slow, read in another translation.

WRITE

Honestly, this is my favorite way to start each morning. I *love* writing out scripture. There's something about the process of handwriting that both wakes me up and allows me to really marinate in the passage. It's also incredibly meaningful to have notebooks filled with handwritten scripture.

IDENTIFY KEY VERSES

In the passage you're reading, which verse holds the nugget of wisdom. Which verses explain the transformation of the main characters. Which verses speak most deeply to you in the season you're in right now?

HIGHLIGHT, UNDERLINE, BRACKET, CIRCLE, JOT

In this digital age, there is something therapeutic about words on a paper page and a pack of highlighters or colored pencils. I always loved looking at my grandmothers Bible filled with highlights, underlines, notes and circles.

Take time to circle commands, underline truths or highlight key verses in your favorite shade of pink. Bible study can be fun and colorful!

OBSERVE

Let your inner Nancy Drew loose. Uncover the 5 W's of the passage. Who, What, When, Where, Why and (don't forget) How. It's amazing how much we can learn from just naming the different elements of a passage or story.

ILLUSTRATE

In the margins of your Bible, or on a HelloMornings worksheet, get creative! Design word art focusing on a key point. Sketch the setting, characters or theme.

OUTLINE

Feeling more cerebral than creative? Outline the story or teaching. Highlight the main points and the sub-points to develop a greater understanding of where the author was coming from and what he was trying to communicate.

PERSONAL PARAPHRASE

Sometimes we learn best by teaching. Imagine you had to share the heart of the passage with a group of friends or a class of children, how would you paraphrase it? Or paraphrase it by incorporating your story into it and the things God has done in your life. You could even paraphrase it by simply incorporating your name in everywhere it has a generic pronoun.

QUESTIONS

Got questions? Just write them down. You can answer them later. Don't let your questions keep you from getting through the passage. Imagine you could interview the author, what would you ask?

RESPOND

A great way to dig deeper into scripture is to as a few simple questions. You can think about the answers as you read or you can write down your responses on the HelloMornings worksheet or in your own journal.

The Bible truly comes alive when we consider and pray about how God wants us to apply it to our own lives.

QUESTIONS TO CONSIDER:
- What does this say about God?
- What does this say about the church?
- What does this say about me?

- What truths are in this passage?
- Does this passage lead me to confess anything in prayer?
- What should I pray?
- What actions should I take?
- How can today be different because of this passage?
- What are some journaling questions?
- What is the lesson from this passage?
- Which key verse should I memorize this week?

RESEARCH

There is so much to be learned on every page of scripture. But sometimes we can take our study to a new level when we start flipping the pages and learning the "story behind the story."

Here are a few things you can research about the passage you are studying.

AUTHOR

Who wrote this passage? What do we know about him and how he fits into the story of the Bible? What were his circumstances? Why did he write it? Who was he writing to? Where was he when he wrote it? What had God done in his life to compel him to write this passage?

BACKGROUND

What was the background of the passage? What story or theme was introduced in previous verses or chapters of the book?

AUDIENCE

Who was the audience that the author was writing to? Why was it written to them? How do you think they responded to it? How would you have responded?

CONTEXT: CULTURAL, HISTORICAL, GRAMMATICAL

What was happening in history at the time the passage was written? What was the culture in which it was written like? How did the culture or the historical circumstances influence the author? Are there any grammatical rhythms or clues identifying or strengthening the authors meaning or ultimate intent?

CROSS REFERENCE

If you have a Bible with cross references (or using an online resource), look up all the verses associated with the passage. What can you learn from them and how do they influence the text?

COMMENTARIES

Read the commentary in your Bible, commentary books or at a trusted online source to gain even more insight into the passage.

TRANSLATIONS

Read the passage in multiple translations. How do they differ? How are they the same? What new truths can you glean from the variety of perspectives?

MAPS

Are there any maps in your Bible or online related to the passage you're studying? Follow the journey of the main characters. Look up modern day pictures of the locations. Research how long their journeys may have taken or any obstacles they may have encountered in their travels (culturally or geographically).

WORD STUDY (ORIGINAL LANGUAGE)

Brush up on your Greek and Hebrew and study the passage in the original language using an interlinear Bible.

READY TO DIVE IN?

Feel free to refer back to this list at any point, but now it's time to dive into the new HelloMornings study.

Here we go...

Cheering you on,

Kat Lee and the *HelloMornings.org* Team

FREE AUDIO VERSION

Email your Amazon receipt to us and get the audio version of this study for free!

Audios@hellomornings.org

INTRODUCTION

Jesus was the Master storyteller. As the Creator of mankind, He knows that we often don't understand or remember a lesson unless we hear it in context. Our hearts and brains are strange that way, aren't they? It's easier to receive instruction when we feel connected to both the storyteller and to the story itself. When we develop a relationship with the characters in the tale, the meaning comes alive. We have an "A-ha!" moment. Scientists say that our whole brains are engaged and activated uniquely when we hear a story. And so, we usually walk away remembering the details.

Throughout the Gospels, Jesus often used stories to convey lessons. That's really all a parable is — a simple story that teaches a spiritual lesson. The writers of the three synoptic Gospels (Matthew, Mark, and Luke), record the parables Jesus told to His followers. John records no specific parables, but does gives us record of other wise sayings, allegories, and figures of speech told in a manner similar to the parables. (See John 10:1-18 for an example.)

Jesus used these parables knowing that some of His listeners would "get it" and some would not. Some would welcome both Him and His teaching. Yet, others would walk away with hardened hearts, still spiritually blind and lost. This was actually a fulfillment of prophecy given in Isaiah. (See Matthew 13:10-17 and Isaiah 6:9-10.) Living on this side of Jesus' death and resurrection, Believers can study the parables to learn powerful truths that can touch our hearts and change our lives.

So in this study, we'll draw together near the feet of our Savior. We'll quiet our hearts and minds as we listen to His words. We'll pray that the message He has for us will penetrate our hearts and accomplish its purpose. And then, we'll ask the Father to water our thirsty souls and let the planted seeds grow into a life changed for His glory.

Do you feel ready for some quiet time with Jesus? Let's gather close and listen to His stories!

Pray with me?

Lord God, thank you for inviting me to draw near my precious Savior's feet. Help me truly listen to Jesus' words and message. Guide me into stillness so these stories penetrate my heart. Reveal any hardened areas and soften them, sweet Lord. I thank you that your words will never return void, but will always accomplish your will. May you be ever glorified in my life as I seek to live to serve you and bring you my humble gift of worship. Amen!

Ali

WEEK ONE
by Ali Shaw

WEEK 1, DAY 1: LUKE 6:46-49

YEARS AGO, MY DAUGHTERS AND I DID A FUN BIBLE STUDY PROJECT. We found a jelly jar and fit a heavy rock inside and placed a tiny, green toy house right on top. It looked quaint — until I poured in the water. The house lifted, then dunked and swirled in the deluge. Later, we taped that same house down to the rock and tried again; it stayed put. My elementary-aged girls got the picture: a house anchored to the rock fares better.

Recently, several tornadoes wound their way through the area where I live and demonstrated a larger scale version of this same physical principle. A friend's cottage was destroyed, while her home built on a concrete foundation was only a little damaged.

Storms in life come inevitably. They may come in the form of actual floods and tornadoes that leave behind destruction and disorder, or they may come in the form of a lost job, a cancer diagnosis, or the death of a loved one. I don't mean to be a pessimist here, but the reality is life will throw some really hard stuff at us. And no matter how physical the storm appears, it always reaches in and affects the spiritual.

Jesus' audience lived in a dry land. Instead of overflowing rivers, many were familiar with gathering from streams threatening to dry. As the trickle died, edging closer to the source of water was natural. But in the quest for something good, one could find unstable territory. And so, the foolish builder in the parable simply established his home right there on an unstable shore. When the rain did come, his house flooded. How foolish to build on sandy soil!

As saved Christians, we've chosen the solid Rock, but the foolish builder can be a warning for us, too. Instead of digging deep into the high Rock of Jesus, are we ever tempted to settle foolishly onto something inferior? Building something beautiful and solid takes effort. Yes, God promises us that our salvation isn't based on works (Ephesians 2:8-9) and that His yoke is easy and His burden is light (Matthew 11:30). But investing in the spiritual disciplines of Bible study and reading, prayer, worship is wise. It isn't always easy to keep a relationship healthy and strong.

When the storms of life come, we can turn up our faces into the torrents with praise, and stand firm on the Rock during the rising tides. Our close relationship with the Rock of Ages will prepare us to weather the storms. After all, a house anchored to the Rock fares better!

— **KEY VERSE** —

...he is like a man building a house, who dug deep and laid the foundation on the rock. (Luke 6:48a)

Hello mornings
God. Plan. Move.

READ : Luke 6:46-49
WRITE : Luke 6:48a

....

....

REFLECT :
- Try to memorize today's key verse.
- Read Luke 6:46. Underline the verbs. Dwell on Jesus' words here.
- How do these verses expound on today's passage? Proverbs 9:1, 14:1, and 1 Corinthians 10:4.
- What does Mark 4:39 remind us about Jesus' power over storms?
- What "shifting sands" might you be drawn to? Personal feelings, popular philosophies, or something else? Pray that God will help you stand firmly on the solid Rock.

RESPOND :

....

....

....

....

....

PLAN TIME

THINGS TO DO (3-5 MAX) :

KEY EVENTS TODAY :

MOVE TIME

MORNING WATER ☐

B : _____
L : _____
D : _____

SNACK :

SIMPLE WORKOUT ☐

I REMEMBER SITTING IN THE PEW LISTENING to a fellow churchgoer's testimony. He cried as he spoke words full of love for Jesus and amazement that God had saved a sordid sinner like him. Though I hadn't always lived obediently, did my own life reflect that same far-reaching love of Christ?

But a few years later, I read about a man who (like me) had sat in a pew, listening to a powerful salvation testimony and began to weep. His wife, misunderstanding his tears, said that yes, God was good to forgive a sinner like that. The husband whispered something like, "No, God is good to reach out to someone like me-- someone who didn't appear to need Him. But in His great grace, he reached in and saved me anyway."

In today's passage, Jesus is at the home of Simon the Pharisee when a sinful woman* enters with an alabaster box of ointment and a heart full of worship. I can imagine the Pharisee leaning against the wall with his arms crossed, grumbling in his mind the words in verse 39. Jesus knew exactly what was going on in Simon's heart and responded with the Parable of the Two Debtors.

The story was simple; Simon was like the debtor who didn't owe much, and the sinful woman was like the one who owed a lot. And when the creditor forgave them both, the one who owed much, loved more. I'll admit, this story confounded me until I realized this: the Pharisee owed much, too. No less than the woman. But in his self-righteousness, he couldn't see that.

Sometimes the biggest hurdle to salvation or in maturing our love for our Savior isn't sins we've committed. It's the sin we don't see. It's the price paid that we shrug off. It's much too easy to become pharisaical and sit in ugly pride and self-righteousness, not seeking forgiveness. But like Jesus explains in the parable, the one who realizes the magnitude of absolution will love much.

Whether our stories sound more like the testimony giver or the husband in my anecdotes, we have all been forgiven much, haven't we? Our response to Jesus should be worshipful love. We are all manner of sinners who owe Him everything. Everything! Though it cost Him so much, He has given so freely. The ransom paid for self-righteous Simon was the same as for the sinful, yet worshipful, woman. All stories can reflect His far-reaching love.

— **KEY VERSE** —

Therefore I tell you, her sins, which are many, are forgiven—for she loved much. But he who is forgiven little, loves little. (Luke 7:47)

*Most scholars agree that there is no Scriptural proof that this was Mary Magdalene. Likewise, there is also no certain evidence to tie this to Mary of Bethany. Likely, this is a separate incident and the woman's name will never be known.

Hello mornings

God. Plan. Move.

READ : Luke 7:36-50
WRITE : Luke 7:47

REFLECT :
- Retell today's parable in your own words.
- Compare Simon's actions with the sinful woman's. (vv. 44-46)
- What insight can Titus 3:5 give us regarding self-righteousness?
- Who do you identify with most in today's passage? Why?
- Let's pray. Lord, unveil our eyes to see the gravity of our sins and love you greatly in return for thesacrifice you've made!.

RESPOND :

PLAN TIME

THINGS TO DO (3-5 MAX) :

KEY EVENTS TODAY :

MOVE TIME

MORNING WATER ☐

B : _____
L : _____
D : _____

SNACK :

SIMPLE WORKOUT ☐

IN SEPTEMBER AND OCTOBER OF 2011, the area where I live was struck by the most destructive wildfire in Texas history. Over 34,000 acres and 1,600 homes were burned. The flames didn't discriminate against anything in its path. Countless friends evacuated their neighborhoods and property not knowing until later if their homes still stood and their possessions remained. After finding out her home burned to the ground, a friend said she wouldn't have done laundry that day if she would've known it would just burn up. We laughed, but I knew it was hard losing everything. I'm glad she knew better than to place her hope and identity in her possessions.

The rich fool in today's parable didn't get that. He was wealthy and had set his mind on gathering together his harvest for his own good pleasure. Verse nineteen tells us that his goal was to "relax, eat, drink, [and] be merry." He hadn't thought about what mattered more, his soul or his possessions. All he had thought was, "What shall I do now?", and that to make room for more, he could just tear down what he already had. Doesn't that seem counterintuitive?

I'd love to be able to look at this rich fool and know I'm nothing like that. Maybe a man chasing a career and a bigger paycheck, a nicer home for his family, and a new sports car could identify more? (Wanting to provide well is not a sin, but covetousness is.) But maybe I am like this. How many times do I look at Pinterest, or magazines, or blog photos, not to simply get ideas, but because I'm dissatisfied with what I have and want better? Do I "pull down my barns" when I'm not being a good steward because I'm distracted by wrong priorities? Or how many times do I feel the need to hoard "just in case." (Wanting to provide isn't a sin, but not trusting God is.)

If I'm honest, I can see some of that rich fool inside of me, and I, too, can heed Jesus' warning. Life is not about the material. Yes, we have to live in a material world, but we don't have to be material girls. Instead, I can be generous toward God and others. I can trust my wonderful Savior to care for me. Faith is so powerful because it's placed in a powerful God who is mighty to save.

My friends who've rebuilt since our wildfire have taught and reminded me of much. Our main concern on this earth is our eternity. We must live with eternal life in mind. And the Way is simple — He is the truth and the life (John 14:6). Jesus tells us not to store up our treasures here, but to store them in Heaven. Like the fool, what we value is shown in our actions. Let's be wise and live showing that we value God above all else!

— KEY VERSE —

And he said to them, "Take care, and be on your guard against all covetousness, for one's life does not consist in the abundance of his possessions.". (Luke 12:15)

Hello mornings

God. Plan. Move.

READ : Luke 12:15-21
WRITE : Luke 12:15

REFLECT :
- For further study, read Luke 12:22-34.
- What did Paul model to the elders of Ephesus regarding living for Christ? (Acts 20:24, 31-35)
- The Laodicean church struggled with valuing the earthly. What does Christ tell them in Revelation 3:17-21?—What tempts you to covet or worry? How can you remove or combat that temptation?
- What does today's passage lead you to pray?

RESPOND :

PLAN TIME

THINGS TO DO (3-5 MAX) :

KEY EVENTS TODAY :

MOVE TIME

MORNING WATER ☐

B : _____
L : _____
D : _____

SNACK :

SIMPLE WORKOUT ☐

WEEK 1, DAY 4: LUKE 12:35-40

I'LL NEVER FORGET THAT SINKING FEELING I HAD WHEN I SAW THE CUT LOCK, dangling from the latch with marks gnawed into the metal. We'd been moving and our shed was the last thing to pack up. While we were settling into our new home in town, someone helped themselves to my husband's tools. Things that he'd been given, things we'd saved for, things we both loved to use — all gone while our interests pulled us the other way.

But thieves come unexpectedly. Looking back, we saw a few things we could have done differently to protect our belongings better. An additional, stronger lock or perhaps even leaving our dog to guard might have made a difference. We learned to be more watchful.

In today's passage, Jesus gives us a spiritual lesson all about being watchful and ready. Ready for what? His return (Luke 12:40). Yet, Pastor Charles Spurgeon and others have used this passage to remind us to prepare for meeting our Savior in death. The day of His return will be the happiest of days for His watchful servants, but will come suddenly like a thief in the night, surprising the unprepared (1 Thessalonians 5:2). Since only God knows the number of our days, our last breath may surprise us, too. Whether for death or His return, we must live spiritually ready.

In verse 35, Jesus says we must be "dressed ready for service" and keep our "lamps burning." In biblical times, people dressed with long outer garments which had to be pulled up and tucked in when it was time to work. And in those days, people carried small, portable lamps to guide them, chase away darkness, and provide protection. Isn't that just what His light does for us? Jesus is telling us that we should be prepared for Him at all times.

I don't always feel ready. Like when breakfast is burning, someone spills milk, and words grow edges, the physical infringes upon the spiritual. But we have a gracious, patient Savior. We can tidy our spiritual houses and be more watchful — trim our wicks and let His light shine bright.

We have a unique relationship with our Lord. Yes, we serve Him - yet not as though He needed anything (Acts 17:25), but He promises us in today's passage that when He finds us ready, He will come and serve us. That's mind blowing, isn't it? Just like He demonstrated in John 13:4-16, Jesus assures us that He will minister to our needs. Our Servant-Savior tells us to be ready. We can't let other interests, good or bad, pull our attention away. Let's live joyfully watchful!

— KEY VERSE —

It will be good for those servants whose master finds them watching when he comes.
(Luke 12:37a, NIV)

GOD TIME

READ : Luke 12:35-40
WRITE : Luke 12:37a

REFLECT :
- Read the passage again, looking for things we should do and things Jesus will do.
- For additional insight, read this parable in Matthew 24:42-44 and Mark 13:32-37.
- What does Jesus say in Mark 10:45? How does He show that in John 13:4-16 and through His death?
- Write down three things you can do today to live spiritually ready.
- How does Christ's superiority make a difference in your life today?
- Pray, thanking Jesus for being a patient, gracious, Servant-Savior. Thank Him that salvation comes by belief in His Son, not works. Praise Him for His great love!

RESPOND :

PLAN TIME

THINGS TO DO (3-5 MAX) :

KEY EVENTS TODAY :

MOVE TIME

MORNING WATER ☐

B : _____
L : _____
D : _____

SNACK :

SIMPLE WORKOUT ☐

ONE ANNIVERSARY, MY HUSBAND REALLY SURPRISED ME. Before leaving the driveway, he turned to me with a blindfold in his hand and said, "You'll need to wear this." The drive seemed long and completely unfamiliar. I felt lost and fearful, yet giddy. Relinquishing control was difficult, but because I had faith in my husband, I just went with it. I knew it would end well. (It did!) And what seemed long and unfamiliar was a well-traveled, 30-minute drive to the city.

Today's passage is a continuation of yesterday's reading. It begins with Peter asking Jesus this question: "Lord, are you telling this parable for us or for all?" You see, Jesus had been speaking to an innumerable crowd (Luke 12:1a), and Peter wants clarification. Was Jesus speaking to the disciples, or everyone? In Peter's typical way, he questions Jesus boldly.

Jesus responds that this parable is for the faithful. According to *John Gill's Exposition of the Entire Bible*:

> "Christ does not directly, and in express words, answer to Peter's question, but suggests, that [though] he intended it as a caution to all his people, and in it spoke to them all to be upon their watch and guard..." —John Gill

So this second half of Jesus' parable of the watchful servants is a reminder to continue on in faithfulness. Jesus tell us that things didn't end well for the servant who "knew His master's will," but didn't prepare faithfully for Him (Luke 12:47). But for those who do prepare faithfully, more opportunities for service will be given (Luke 12:48, Luke 19:17, and Matthew 25:21).

When the Israelites traveled to the Promised Land, God led them by covering the tabernacle with a cloud by day and a pillar of fire by night. When the cloud lifted, the Israelites packed up and faithfully followed it. They showed faith in the waiting, watching, and following, much like in the parable Jesus told. Ultimately, it isn't the work that Jesus was commending, it's the faith. After all, faith is credited to us as righteousness. (Genesis 15:6, Romans 4:22-25)

It can seem like we have no control over where God takes us and how long it takes to get there. We pray, we wait, and sometimes we question. Sometimes we don't feel His presence. But the fact is, He promises to "never leave nor forsake us." (Deuteronomy 31:6) Because we have full faith in our loving God, we can rest assured knowing things will end well. How wonderful!

— **KEY VERSE** —

And the Lord said, "Who then is the faithful and wise manager, whom his master will set over his household, to give them their portion of food at the proper time?" (Luke 12:42)

GOD TIME

READ : Luke 12:41-48
WRITE : Luke 12:42

. . . .

. . . .

REFLECT :
- What would you choose to be the key verse for this passage? Why?
- Read all the verses listed in parentheses in today's commentary.
- Verse 42 uses the word "wise." Why do you think Jesus added this condition to faithfulness?
- What's the hardest part of following God faithfully? Using a concordance, find verses for encouragement.
- Thank God that He is trustworthy, loving, and good. Thank Him for leading you.

RESPOND :

. . . .

. . . .

. . . .

. . . .

PLAN TIME

THINGS TO DO (3-5 MAX) :

KEY EVENTS TODAY :

MOVE TIME

MORNING WATER ☐

B : _____

L : _____

D : _____

SNACK :

SIMPLE WORKOUT ☐

WEEK 2, DAY 1: LUKE 13:6-9

I HAVE ALWAYS BEEN FASCINATED WITH FARMING. Growing up, my father worked as a produce merchandiser for a local grocery store. He would visit the farms and bring home countless samples of delicious fruits and vegetables. We loved it! To my dad, farming was a business. If a farm failed to produce a quality product, it not only cost the farm money, but it would cost my dad's company money as well. From a farmer's perspective, a plant that failed to produce was simply a waste of time and land.

Throughout His ministry, Jesus told many parables involving plants and farming. Not only was agriculture a relevant topic at the time of Christ, but on numerous occasions in the Old Testament, vineyards and trees were images God used to illustrate His relationship with His people. An example of this is found in Isaiah 5 where God reveals Himself to be a vineyard owner, while the vineyard is none other than "the house of Israel."

It is no secret that Jesus was frustrated with the Jewish religious leaders. He called them hypocrites on numerous occasions and made it abundantly clear that judgment was coming. The Pharisees were lost in their pride. They truly believed that their ancestry was enough to save them. They outwardly followed the rules, but their hearts did not belong to God. This fig tree illustrated the truth. God's people produce godly fruit, and many of the Jewish people were lacking in fruit production.

We see this clearly illustrated when John the Baptist is speaking to the Pharisees in Matthew 3:7-10. He tells them not to assume they are saved by the fact that they are descendants of Abraham. God is looking for fruit-bearers. *"Even now the axe is laid to the root of the trees..."* (Matthew 3:10) John the Baptist was warning them of what would come if they refused to repent.

As I read this parable, I can't help but be reminded of Jesus' words. *"I am the vine; you are the branches. Whoever abides in me and I in him, he it is that bears much fruit, for apart from me you can do nothing."* (John 15:5) Jesus made it clear throughout His ministry that He is the only way to the Father. Outward law-abiding and ancestry have nothing to do with our salvation. It is through Christ alone that we can be saved. And once we are saved, we can be fruitful as we grow and abide in Him.

— **KEY VERSE** —

And he told this parable: "A man had a fig tree planted in his vineyard, and he came seeking fruit on it and found none." (Luke 13:6)

Hello mornings

God. Plan. Move.

READ : Luke 13:6-9
WRITE : Luke 13:6

....

....

REFLECT :
- According to Luke 13:5, what would have caused the fig tree to produce fruit?
- Why did the vinedresser ask to wait one year before removing the tree? (see 2 Peter 3:9)
- The vinedresser took time to nurture the tree before cutting it down. What does this reveal about God and His mercy?
- Read Galatians 5:22-23 and Colossians 1:9-12. What are some examples of godly fruit?
- Jesus is the True Vine. Describe in your own words what it means to "abide" in Him.

RESPOND :

....

....

....

....

....

PLAN TIME

THINGS TO DO (3-5 MAX) :

KEY EVENTS TODAY :

MOVE TIME

MORNING WATER ☐

B : _____

L : _____

D : _____

SNACK :

SIMPLE WORKOUT ☐

WEEK 2, DAY 2: MATTHEW 13:3-8, 18-23

HAVE YOU EVER BEEN HIT WITH NEWS THAT TOOK SOME TIME TO PROCESS?
I remember the day I found out that I was pregnant with my oldest daughter. My husband and I had been praying for this moment for quite some time, yet when it finally happened, I was caught off guard. It was not until I saw her first ultrasound that the news took root in my heart.

The good news of the Gospel is just that – good news! And as amazing as the news of my daughter was to me and my husband, it is nothing compared to the good news of Jesus and salvation. Today's parable is perhaps one of the most well-known stories Jesus ever told. We encounter one kind of seed, yet four types of soil.

Unlike many of His other parables, Jesus offers an explanation to His disciples about this one. The seed being planted is the Gospel. It is the good news of salvation! But each of the four soils responds to this news differently.

The seed sown along the path never takes root. It is snatched away by the enemy before it ever has the chance. The rocky ground receives the Gospel with joy and excitement. Inability to take root, however, causes the plant to wither at the first sign of trials. The thorns also receive the seed, but worries and worldly wealth choke the Word and the plants fail to produce fruit. In the end, it is the good soil that receives the truth with joy and yields a plant that can produce much fruit.

If you have been a Christian for long, you have undoubtedly heard this parable. The concept is simple; we should all strive to be the good soil. On a personal level, I must admit that I am not always the best at being "good soil." I strive to be, but sometimes I am weak and struggling with trials like the rocky ground. Other times I am like the thorny soil. I worry about life instead of surrendering my circumstances to God.

In this parable, Jesus was not only outlining four types of people who would hear His Word, but He was also sharing with us the secret to producing godly fruit. The good soil not only hears the Word, but applies it. We allow it to sink deeply into our hearts and take root.

— KEY VERSE —

As for what was sown on good soil, this is the one who hears the word and understands it. He indeed bears fruit and yields, in one case a hundredfold, in another sixty, and in another thirty. (Matthew 13:23)

Hello mornings

God. Plan. Move.

READ : Matthew 13:3-8, 18-23
WRITE : Matthew 13:23

....

....

REFLECT :
- According to Matthew 7:18-19, is it possible to be saved and not produce good fruit?
- Which of the four soils received the Good News and found salvation in Christ?
- What additional truths about the good soil do we find in Luke 8:15?
- It is a person's heart that determines whether the seed will take root and grow. How does this encourage you as you share the Gospel?
- What roles do love and servanthood play in softening the hearts of the world around us?

RESPOND :

....

....

....

....

....

....

PLAN TIME

THINGS TO DO (3-5 MAX) :

KEY EVENTS TODAY :

MOVE TIME

MORNING WATER ☐

B : _____
L : _____
D : _____

SNACK :

SIMPLE WORKOUT ☐

WEEK 2, DAY 3: MATTHEW 13:24-30, 36-43

I WILL NEVER FORGET THE DAY my daughter ate her first chocolate-covered espresso bean. It was quite traumatic! You see, my 3-year-old absolutely loves chocolate-covered raisins. And since she cannot read yet, she mistook her daddy's espresso beans for her mommy's raisins. She was sobbing from the shock, but she learned an important lesson that day. Things are not always what they appear to be on the outside.

In the parable of the wheat and weeds (some translations use the word "tares"), Jesus describes two types of seed growing side by side. In verse 37 we discover that the one sowing the good seed is Jesus, and His seed refers to the "sons of the kingdom." The weeds, however, are sown by the enemy and represent "sons of the evil one."

The most interesting aspect of this parable is not the fact that there are sons of God and sons of the evil one co-living in the world. Looking at the world today, this truth is clearly seen. It is the fact that they are purposely allowed to grow together.

Many scholars believe that the weeds in this passage are referring to "darnel," which is a type of weed that looks very similar to wheat. In fact, they look so alike in their early stages that darnel is sometimes referred to as "false wheat." It is extremely difficult to tell them apart until they are fully developed. And once they are fully developed, their roots are so intertwined that you must harvest them together before taking the time to separate them one by one.

Because the wheat and the weeds look the same in their infancy, we need to be careful as the church to protect and care for the entire field. What you mistake for a weed today, may in fact be wheat that isn't fully mature yet. We are called to love another as Christ loved us and to pray for our enemies.

On the other hand, what you believe to be wheat may turn out to be a weed. For this reason, it is crucial that we rely on the Holy Spirit and God's Word in discerning truth. False teachers have a way of appearing like wheat before the truth comes to light.

One of my favorite aspects of this parable is that what you see on the surface may not be an indication of what is going on inside. Just like the wheat and the weeds grow together and appear the same, we never know what God is doing in the hearts of those around us.

— **KEY VERSE** —

Then the righteous will shine like the sun in the kingdom of their Father. He who has ears, let him hear. (Matthew 13:43)

GOD TIME

READ : Matthew 13:24-30, 36-43
WRITE : Matthew 13:43

. . . .

. . . .

REFLECT :
- What ultimately happens to the weeds in this parable?
- What promise do we receive as God's "wheat" in Matthew 13:43?
- Read Matthew 7:21-22. What do we learn about outward appearances?
- Read 1 John 3:9-10. What additional truths do we learn from this passage about the sons of God and the sons of the devil?
- According to 1 John 5:18-20, how can we know for certain that we belong to God?

RESPOND :

. . . .

. . . .

. . . .

. . . .

. . . .

PLAN TIME

THINGS TO DO (3-5 MAX) :

KEY EVENTS TODAY :

MOVE TIME

MORNING WATER ☐

B : _____
L : _____
D : _____

SNACK :

SIMPLE WORKOUT ☐

WEEK 2, DAY 4: MARK 4:26-29

WE'VE ALL BEEN THERE...THAT AWKWARD MOMENT when you want to share Jesus with someone but you can't seem to find the words. What should I say? What if I just push them away or they get angry with me? It can be hard to find the courage to say something. And when we do find the strength, we struggle with what to say and how to say it.

We all have people in our lives that we long to see come to Jesus. We pray and hope believing that one day they see the truth for themselves. In His parable of the seed growing, Jesus gives us hope as believers. He identifies a spiritual truth that we can rely on.

This short parable may not seem like much on the surface, but it illustrates an amazing truth about how God is growing His kingdom. Not everything is up to us. There is a supernatural, spiritual aspect to kingdom growing that only God can accomplish. A man scatters seed, and *"the seed sprouts and grows; he knows not how."* (Mark 4:27)

Our job is to scatter seed. Jesus made this truth clear when He gave us the Great Commission to go into the world and share the Good News with everyone. But we are not responsible for the seed's growth. Only God can cause a seed to sprout. We plant, water, and tend to the seeds; but it is God who supernaturally causes the seed to grow.

"So neither he who plants nor he who waters is anything, but only God who gives the growth." (1 Corinthians 3:7) I find this truth to be rather comforting. It is not up to me to create growth. When I share the truth with a loved one, I am able to put that seed into the hands of God. It is not about saying the right thing at the right time, but rather to speak the truth and to surrender the rest to the Holy Spirit. Even the most eloquent of speeches cannot change a person's heart. Only God is capable of that.

As God's Kingdom grows, we have a role to play. We have spiritual seed to scatter. It may be God that changes hearts, but He uses us in the process. What a wonderful blessing it is to be a part of God's plan! We have the privilege to scatter seed and watch as God turns it into something beautiful. It is a privilege that we should never take lightly.

— **KEY VERSE** —

But when the grain is ripe, at once he puts in the sickle, because the harvest has come. (Mark 4:29)

Hello mornings

God. Plan. Move.

READ : Mark 4:26-29
WRITE : Mark 4:29

. . . .

. . . .

REFLECT :
- What do we learn about spiritual growth in Mark 4:28 and how can we apply that to our witnessing?
- Who is the "he" in Mark 4:29 and what does this say about our role in Kingdom growth?
- Think of someone in your life who needs Jesus. Pray and ask for wisdom in knowing when to scatter seed and when to surrender their growth to God.
- What promise do we receive for being willing to scatter seed in 1 Corinthians 3:8-9?
- Read 1 Corinthians 3:10-15. What additional truths do we learn about spiritual growth?

RESPOND :

. . . .

. . . .

. . . .

. . . .

. . . .

PLAN TIME

THINGS TO DO (3-5 MAX) :

KEY EVENTS TODAY :

MOVE TIME

MORNING WATER ☐

B : _____
L : _____
D : _____

SNACK :

SIMPLE WORKOUT ☐

WEEK 2, DAY 5: MATTHEW 13:31-33

I REMEMBER THE ONE TIME MY FAMILY MOVED WHEN I WAS GROWING UP. We were building a new home, and I loved imagining all the possibilities as our home took shape. One of the main aspects I remember most, however, is the yard – or perhaps the lack thereof. My family spent that first summer planting grass and landscaping. We planted several small trees that looked more like twigs with leaves than actual trees. Over two decades later, our "twigs with leaves" have became beautiful trees that provide their front yard with plenty of shade.

A mustard seed is small. When held in one's hand, it seems unlikely to produce anything substantial. But we all know what can happen when a seed is planted in good soil. Commentators often disagree with the exact meaning behind this parable, but most say that the seed represents the Kingdom of God and that it is ever growing and expanding.

The Kingdom certainly had small beginnings. A handful of men chosen by Jesus went out into the world leading to what is now the largest religion in the world. Statistically speaking, about one-third of the world bows the knee to Jesus as their Lord and Savior.

When it comes to identifying the birds, scholars vary in their interpretations. Who are they? And what does it mean that they are found lodging in the tree's branches?

First of all, the tree is big enough to house them and provide them shade. This is important because mustard seeds generally produce very small trees. The fact that this tree is so large speaks to the supernatural aspect of God's Kingdom. His Kingdom will not be defined by our worldly standards. Secondly, the tree is perceived as a safe haven. The birds may not be a part of God's Kingdom, but they know that they can find shelter in its branches.

Immediately following this parable, Jesus tells a story about yeast. In comparison to the other ingredients, yeast seems small and insignificant; but it is the yeast that causes the bread to rise. It starts small and works through the entire batch of dough.

I do not think it is a coincidence that Jesus told these stories side by side. Both identify the small beginnings of His Kingdom, and they both demonstrate its growth. When the disciples felt discouraged as they began sharing the Gospel, they could recall these stories of hope. God would turn their efforts into something amazing.

— **KEY VERSE** —

It is the smallest of all seeds, but when it has grown it is larger than all the garden plants and becomes a tree, so that the birds of the air come and make nests in its branches. (Matthew 13:32)

Hello mornings
God. Plan. Move.

READ : Matthew 13:31-33
WRITE : Matthew 13:32

....

....

....

REFLECT :
- Read Luke 17:5-6. What else does Jesus liken to a mustard seed?
- In a prayer journal, describe how these parables encourage you as you grow in the Lord.
- Read Mark 4:30-32 and Luke 13:18-21. What additional truths do we learn?
- Read Ezekiel 17:22-24. Compare this passage with the parable of the mustard seed.
- Describe how these parables would have encouraged the disciples in their small beginnings as the church.

RESPOND :

....

....

....

....

....

....

PLAN TIME

THINGS TO DO (3-5 MAX) :

KEY EVENTS TODAY :

MOVE TIME

MORNING WATER ☐

B : _____

L : _____

D : _____

SNACK :

SIMPLE WORKOUT ☐

WEEK 3, DAY 1: 1 MATTHEW 13:44-50

MY EIGHT-YEAR-OLD SON LOVES TO COLLECT THINGS. Last weekend, after staying all night with my parents, he came home with a couple of trash bags full of items he found lying on the side of the road. He had an old volleyball my mom told me had been near her house for about six months. He also had about 15 feathers, a beat up frisbee, some pinecones, and a huge multi- colored rock he is convinced has gold inside of it.

My husband and I have a relatively small home and don't like clutter, so I wasn't thrilled when I saw all the junk he came home with. My first thought was, "We are NOT going to keep all of this stuff."

The more I thought about it, though, the more I realized I couldn't throw it out. The truth is, even though to me it looked like junk, to him, it was a treasure. The items became valuable because they held value in my son's eyes.

In today's passage of Scripture, Jesus told three parables. The first two parables speak clearly about the value of the kingdom of heaven. The first parable tells the story of a man who found a hidden treasure in a field and was so thrilled about the treasure he sold everything he had and bought the field. The second parable is similar. It tells the story of a merchant who was searching for pearls. When he found a valuable one, he sold everything he had and bought that pearl.

The meaning of these two parables is the same. The kingdom of heaven is so valuable it's worth giving up everything for. Money is worthless when compared to the kingdom of heaven. So is fame, success, and the stuff of this world. Following Jesus might cost us. (See Luke 14:25-33.) But the kingdom we gain as a result of following him is worth the cost.

When my son brought home those items, he valued them. He wouldn't allow his younger brother to hold them for fear of him breaking them. He put them in a safe place and took care of them. My question to us today is this: are we placing as much value on the kingdom of heaven as my son placed on his "treasure"? Or, are we treating it like nothing more than junk found on the side of the road?

— **KEY VERSE** —

The kingdom of heaven is like treasure hidden in a field, which a man found and covered up. Then in his joy he goes and sells all that he has and buys that field. (Matthew 13:44)

Hello mornings

God. Plan. Move.

READ : Matthew 13:44-50
WRITE : Matthew 13:44

REFLECT :
- Read Philippians 3:7-8. How does this verse relate to today's passage of Scripture?
- Paraphrase the three parables in this text.
- Is there anything in your life you are valuing more than God?
- Read through the text again and underline any words that show how valuable the kingdom of heaven is. (i.e. treasure, joy, etc.)
- Memorize Philippians 3:7.

RESPOND :

PLAN TIME

THINGS TO DO (3-5 MAX) :

KEY EVENTS TODAY :

MOVE TIME

MORNING WATER ☐

B : _____
L : _____
D : _____

SNACK :

SIMPLE WORKOUT ☐

WHEN I PICKED UP MY SON FROM HIS CLASS AT THE Y THIS MORNING, his teachers said he had a rough time. "He and another child don't get along … We had to separate them again." If you're a parent, you know the disappointment I felt. No parent wants to hear that their child isn't being kind. On the way home, as I talked to my son about loving our neighbors, God brought to mind today's parable.

The characters in this story likely had many reasons not to help the hurt man, just as my son claimed he had reasons not to be kind to the child in his class. Nonetheless, Jesus' point in telling this parable was that we should put aside our excuses and be kind anyway.

Let's look at this parable in detail. Here are the characters of the story: a man who is hurt by robbers, a priest, a Levite, and a Samaritan. The priest, Levite, and Samaritan all passed by the hurt man. Each of them likely had good reasons NOT to stop and help. Maybe they feared the robbers would hurt them, too. Maybe they were already running late. Maybe they had important work to do. For the Samaritan, he could have easily avoided helping because of the long-seated hatred between Jews and Samaritans.

What's amazing about this parable, though, is that the Samaritan did stop. He put aside his excuses and saw the man for what he really was: a person needing love. The robbers viewed the man as someone to hurt. The priest and Levite viewed him as someone to avoid. But the Samaritan viewed him properly.

I wonder how I would have viewed him. Would I have viewed him as an interruption in my day? Would I have viewed him as a problem I didn't want to deal with? Would I have viewed him as someone who was going to cost me time and money? Or would I, like the Samaritan, have viewed him as a person who needed love?

Loving our neighbors isn't always convenient. Sometimes, it means we have to rearrange our schedules or dish out cash like the Samaritan did. Other times, it means we have to be kind to someone who isn't kind to us.

Loving our neighbor means seeing them for who they really are: people needing love. I hope my son is beginning to learn this lesson, and I hope I am, too.

— KEY VERSE —

And he answered, "You shall love the Lord your God with all your heart and with all your soul and with all your strength and with all your mind, and your neighbor as yourself." (Luke 10:27)

GOD TIME

READ : Luke 10:29-42
WRITE : Luke 10:27

REFLECT :
- Read Deuteronomy 6:5 and Leviticus 19:18. How do these verses relate to today's text?
- Which of the characters in this text do you relate to most and why?
- Considering the culture, why was it so shocking that the Samaritan helped the man?
- Sketch the story, drawing each of the main characters as you picture them in your mind.
- As a result of reading this parable, is there anything you need to confess to God? Is there anyone you haven't loved well?

RESPOND :

PLAN TIME

THINGS TO DO (3-5 MAX) :

KEY EVENTS TODAY :

MOVE TIME

MORNING WATER ☐

B : _____
L : _____
D : _____

SNACK :

SIMPLE WORKOUT ☐

WEEK 3, DAY 3: LUKE 11:5-10

HAVE YOU EVER PRAYED FOR SOMETHING FOR YEARS, only to hear silence from God in response to your pleas? This has been my story for the past six years. My husband and I long for another child and have asked God repeatedly over the years to grant us that request. Instead of a healthy baby, though, we have experienced four miscarriages.

So when I read verses like these in Luke 11, I can easily grow discouraged. How can verse 9 that says "ask, and it will be given to you" be reconciled with my personal experiences? Maybe you, too, have felt as though your prayers landed on deaf ears. Maybe you, too, have wondered if it was worth it to keep praying?

This passage of Scripture reminds us there's value in persistence in prayer. Let's back up a little bit, though, and look at the context to understand the meaning of the parable.

At the beginning of chapter 11, Jesus was praying. When He finished, one of His disciples asked Him to teach them to pray. In response to this request, Jesus told them the Lord's Prayer and then moved into the parable we are studying today.

In this parable, a man came to his friend at midnight and asked the friend to lend him some bread for a guest staying at his home. The friend refused, saying he and his family were already in bed. The man boldly continued to ask, though, until the friend finally got up and gave the man what he needed.

Jesus did not share this parable so we would picture God like a man who doesn't want to be bothered. Not every single detail in Jesus' parables serves as a direct comparison to something else. In this case, the comparison was meant to be between the asking man and us, encouraging us to ask boldly and continuously just as the man did. The comparison ends there. Jesus did not intend us to compare the unconcerned homeowner with God.

Jesus shared this parable to encourage his followers to be persistent in their prayers. Don't ask one time and then stop asking, He told them. Keep asking. Keep knocking. Keep seeking. Because if there's one thing I have learned in the past six years, it's that there's value in persistence in prayer. God may not give you everything you ask Him for, but He'll use your asking to build you into the person He longs for you to become.

—  —

And I tell you, ask, and it will be given to you; seek, and you will find; knock, and it will be opened to you. (Luke 11:9)

Hello mornings
God. Plan. Move.

READ : Luke 11:5-10
WRITE : Luke 11:9

REFLECT :
  – Read Luke 18:1-8. How is this parable similar to today's text? How is it different?
  – What is the primary lesson Jesus was teaching his disciples through this parable?
  – What does this parable teach us about ourselves? About prayer?
  – Read a parallel passage in Matthew 7:7-8.
  – How does Christ's superiority make a difference in your life today?
  – Spend a few moments in prayer, persistently asking God for the needs and desires of your heart.

RESPOND :

PLAN TIME

THINGS TO DO (3-5 MAX) :

KEY EVENTS TODAY :

MOVE TIME

MORNING WATER ☐

B : _____
L : _____
D : _____

SNACK :

SIMPLE WORKOUT ☐

WHEN I WAS IN HIGH SCHOOL, I STRUGGLED A LOT WITH INSECURITY. I often felt like I wasn't good enough or pretty enough or skinny enough or whatever-enough. Part of the reason I struggled so much was I refused to recognize the good qualities in myself. Instead, I practiced a form of "false humility." I thought I was being humble by putting myself down, but I wasn't.

True humility is not thinking poorly of yourself. Instead, as C.S. Lewis said so well, *"True humility is not thinking less of yourself; it is thinking of yourself less."* When I constantly focused on my negative qualities, I was still constantly focused on myself. True humility is learning to think of others instead. It's not putting yourself down but refusing to think about yourself at all.

Jesus painted a good picture of humility in the parable in Luke 14. In this story, Jesus told about a wedding feast. He said, "When you are invited by someone to a wedding feast, do not sit down in a place of honor, lest someone more distinguished than you be invited by him" (Luke 14:8). If you do this, Jesus added, the host will ask you to move to a less distinguished seat and bring shame upon you.

In Jesus' culture, shame and honor were even more important than they are today, so you can imagine how humiliating it would be if this actually happened. Instead of taking the most important seat, Jesus challenged his followers to take the least important seat. That way, the host could exalt you in front of his guests by asking you to move up to a more important place.

The application to this parable is clear. Jesus is calling all of his followers to behave in humility. He's asking us to think of others instead of thinking about ourselves and to lift up other people instead of lifting up ourselves.

He's not asking us to put ourselves down, but to instead recognize who we are in the eyes of our Father and, because we know who we are, stop seeking affirmation from others. We don't need other people to exalt us so we feel good about ourselves because we are children of the Most High God.

In essence, when we walk into a room, we shouldn't need to be noticed, because we know we have already been noticed by our Father in Heaven. And that, my friends, is enough recognition for us to be fully satisfied.

— KEY VERSE —

For everyone who exalts himself will be humbled, and he who humbles himself will be exalted. (Luke 14:11)

GOD TIME

READ : Luke 14:7-14
WRITE : Luke 14:11

. . . .

. . . .

REFLECT :
- Read Proverbs 25:6-7. How does this proverb relate to today's parable?
- Read Philippians 2:1-11. How did Jesus display humility in His life on this earth?
- What is the primary lesson from this parable?
- What does humility look like on a day-to-day basis?
- Read Matthew 23:1-12. What are the similarities and differences between this passage and our text today from Luke?

RESPOND :

. . . .

. . . .

. . . .

. . . .

PLAN TIME

THINGS TO DO (3-5 MAX) :

KEY EVENTS TODAY :

MOVE TIME

MORNING WATER ☐

B : _____
L : _____
D : _____

SNACK :

SIMPLE WORKOUT ☐

I READ A STORY RECENTLY ON FACEBOOK about a little boy who had a birthday party and no one came. It broke my heart thinking of how that little boy must have felt as he waited for his friends to arrive and as he eventually realized no one was coming.

Shortly after reading that story, my son celebrated his birthday. Unfortunately, a large snow and ice storm hit our area the day before his party. My husband and I struggled to decide if we should cancel his party or not.

"What if we have the party, and no one shows?" I asked him. Thankfully, that didn't happen. We had the party and, though some of his friends couldn't come because of the weather, he still had many who could.

In today's text, Jesus told a parable about a man who threw a feast that few wanted to attend. The man invited many guests. Then, as was customary in that time period, he sent a second invitation when the banquet was ready. *"Come, for everything is now ready,"* he told them in verse 17. One by one, each of the guests made excuses as to why they couldn't come. One said he needed to see a field he had just purchased. Another said he needed to try out his oxen. One was newly married.

When the servant told the man what the guests said, the man told the servant to go into the streets and bring in anyone who would come. *"Bring in the poor and crippled and blind and lame,"* he told his servant in Luke 14:21. He wanted his house to be full, so the servant followed his master's orders and filled the banquet. But not one of those who made excuses was allowed to come in.

Just as the man called on the guests to come to his banquet, God invites us to come into His kingdom. I'm afraid, though, that just as the guests had excuses, we often do, too. The guests in the parable didn't come because of work obligations and family responsibilities. The timing wasn't ideal for them, so they turned down the invitation. Many of us resist God's call on our lives for the same reasons. It's inconvenient. It interferes with work or family.

The truth is, there is nothing more important in our lives than God's invitation. And this invitation is definitely one we want to accept.

— **KEY VERSE** —

When one of those who reclined at table with him heard these things, he said to him, "Blessed is everyone who will eat bread in the kingdom of God!" (Luke 14:15)

GOD TIME

READ : Luke 14:15-24
WRITE : Luke 14:15

....

....

....

REFLECT :
- What are some excuses people might make today to put off accepting Jesus' call?
- Is there any excuse you have been making that you need to confess today?
- Read Revelation 19:9. How does this verse relate to today's parable?
- What does this parable teach us about God?
- Thinking of the context, who was Jesus likely referring to when He spoke of the "poor, crippled, blind, and lame"? Who was He referring to as the invited guests?

RESPOND :

....

....

....

....

....

....

PLAN TIME

THINGS TO DO (3-5 MAX) :

KEY EVENTS TODAY :

MOVE TIME

MORNING WATER ☐

B : _____

L : _____

D : _____

SNACK :

SIMPLE WORKOUT ☐

WEEK FOUR
by Cheli Sigler

WEEK 4, DAY 1: LUKE 14:25-33

AS THE CROWDS PRESS CLOSE TO HEAR JESUS, there is no slick salesman talk to gain a few followers. Journeying to Jerusalem, Jesus makes it known that He wants men and women who will follow Him all the way to the cross—disciples who strive to be like Him in word and action, so the world will know that He is "the way, the truth, and the life" (John 14:6).

Using two brief examples, building a tower or assembling an army for war, He makes clear that the costs must be considered or failure is assured. Likewise, Jesus wants me to know from the outset, that being His disciple isn't easy, but the work of discipleship will have its full effect of making me "perfect and complete, lacking in nothing" (James 4:4) when I enter eternity.

First Jesus tells the crowd, *"whoever does not carry their cross and follow me cannot be my disciple."* (Luke 14:27) To carry my cross, I look to Jesus for my example:

"... Jesus, the founder and perfecter of our faith, who for the joy that was set before him endured the cross, despising the shame..." (Hebrews 12:2)

The cross put to death Christ's physical body, making Jesus the sacrifice for my sin. (2 Corinthians 5:21) The Holy Spirit uses the cross of motherhood to put to death pride and self-reliance in me. I must carry my cross, so I can experience the depth of my Savior's love, mercy, and grace.

Jesus also teaches in today's passage that a disciple gives up everything: *"If anyone comes to me and does not hate father and mother...—yes, even their own life—such a person cannot be my disciple."* (Luke 14:26) The Greek the word for "hate" is miséo (3404). The meaning of the word in this passage is "to love someone or something less than someone (something) else" or "to renounce one choice in favor of another." There are innumerable things that distract and tempt me away from Him. "Family first" is a common mantra, but Jesus asks me to make Him my first priority.

Just as Jesus kept moving toward the cross, I need to remember that discipleship is a journey. Daily, the Holy Spirit contends for me, correcting and instructing me to stay on the path. God knows I am human; He makes a way for me that rejoices in my progress without requiring my perfection.

— **KEY VERSE** —

In the same way, those of you who do not give up everything you have cannot be my disciples. (Luke 14:33)

GOD TIME

READ : Luke 14:25-33
WRITE : Luke 14:33

. . . .

. . . .

REFLECT :
- Conduct a word study on the word "disciple." What did you learn?
- Have you ever considered the cost of following Jesus? Why or why not?
- What is your cross to bear? How does it make you more like Jesus?
- What is the Holy Spirit asking you to give up so you can focus on your life with Christ? Chart your discipleship journey. What is your next step?

RESPOND :

. . . .

. . . .

. . . .

. . . .

. . . .

PLAN TIME

THINGS TO DO (3-5 MAX) :

KEY EVENTS TODAY :

MOVE TIME

MORNING WATER ☐

B : _____
L : _____
D : _____

SNACK :

SIMPLE WORKOUT ☐

WEEK 4, DAY 2: LUKE 15:8-10

"I LOST MY KEYS IN THE GREAT UNKNOWN...." You might be singing that Francesca Battistelli song with me right now; it could be my theme song. Not too long ago my husband lost our car keys. He searched the trash can (the big, smelly one) three times, only to find them a week later in someone's sneaker. What a laugh and celebration we had! In the parable of the lost coin, I am reminded that God loves all lost people, and even better—finding them.

Whether a day's wage or an ornament marking her marital status, the silver coin (one of ten), was of utmost value to the woman in Jesus' story. Every person has value to God: *"Look at the birds of the air; they neither sow nor reap...yet your heavenly Father feeds them. Are you not of more value than they?"* (Matthew 6:26). A play titled, Nothing is Lost That Can't Be Found! could easily be a banner in heaven-eternal home of the found. There is no one that God wants left from His care. As a disciple of Jesus, I want to cultivate a heart for the lost like Jesus.

In order to find the coin, the woman had to light a lamp and sweep the house. Among the dusty floors of this small and likely windowless home, is the small coin. Jesus is the *"light of the world"* (John 8:12); He brings the light of truth to the mess. Jesus wasn't afraid to engage those lost in sin; He came to seek them out and save them. (Luke 19:10) I can't say that I'm excited to go into the dark, dirty places and engage the world for Jesus' sake, but as a disciple I am willing to let the Holy Spirit guide me and pray for opportunities.

When the coin is found, its formerly lost status makes it even more valuable. Celebration erupts. Likewise, in heaven, rejoicing erupts as the one who lived separated from God repents, and turns to live a life with God.

The Lord your God is in your midst, a mighty one who will save; he will rejoice over you with gladness...he will exult over you with loud singing. (Zephaniah 3:17)

According to the culture of the day, it was more likely that Jesus' skeptics and scoffers would have rejoiced over the condemnation of a sinner than his restoration. As a disciple of Jesus, I pray that my heart is soft and open to welcome all sinners who repent.

— KEY VERSE —

Just so, I tell you, there is joy before the angels of God over one sinner who repents. (Luke 15:10)

GOD TIME

READ : Luke 15:8-10
WRITE : Luke 15:10

. . . .

. . . .

REFLECT :
  – Research the Greek word for "coin" in Luke 15:8 and the value to the woman in the parable.
  – Make a list of 3-5 verses on an index card that affirm your value to God. Review it frequently.
  – Spend time in prayer praying for lost people you know.
  – Make a list of ministries in your church that conduct outreach to your community.
  – Pray, and ask God to give you opportunities to seek and reach the lost.

RESPOND :

. . . .

. . . .

. . . .

. . . .

. . . .

PLAN TIME

THINGS TO DO (3-5 MAX) :

KEY EVENTS TODAY :

MOVE TIME

MORNING WATER ☐

B : _____

L : _____

D : _____

SNACK :

SIMPLE WORKOUT ☐

WEEK 4, DAY 3: MATTHEW 18:10-14

PRIOR TO TELLING TODAY'S PARABLE, THE LOST SHEEP, Jesus tangled with tax collectors and reprimanded The Twelve for arguing over which of them would be the greatest in God's kingdom. The story of the lost sheep might step on their toes a bit.

On the heels of His disciples arguing who is greater, Jesus calls out their pride, and commands them not to look down on these "little ones." In this passage, "little ones" could refer to young children, but probably also to those who have childlike faith. (Matthew 18:3) God's care and protection for His saints includes the help of angels (Matthew 18:10) and most likely the types of angels described in Hebrews 1:14: *"Are they not all ministering spirits sent out to serve for the sake of those who are to inherit salvation?"*

The parable features God as the shepherd and Believers as the flock of sheep in the shepherd's care. God provides safe refuge and protection for those who love Him and believe in Him (Psalm 91:4). As a disciple of Jesus, I am called to respect those He loves, especially brothers and sisters in Christ: *"encourage one another and build one another up, just as you are doing."* (1 Thessalonians 5:11)

As much as God cares for them, sheep wander away. It breaks God's heart to have one His beloved fall to temptation and stray outside His protection. Even when it's one sheep out of a hundred, our shepherd-God leaves the ninety-nine to find the one who left the fold. Pastor Charles Spurgeon said of believers who have strayed, *"We must not wait till we see some better thing in them, but feel an intense interest for them as what they are— straying and lost."* As a disciple of Jesus, I honor God and learn to care for others as He does by extending forgiveness and grace because I have been forgiven; *"Be kind to one another, tenderhearted, forgiving one another, as God in Christ forgave you."* (Ephesians 4:32)

When the lost are found, just as with the lost coin, there is rejoicing. Luke 5:13 even mentions the heightened sense of joy over the one stray than the ninety-nine who remained. God loves us individually—despite the millions of people on the earth—He takes joy in you.

You prepare a table before me in the presence of my enemies; you anoint my head with oil; my cup overflows. (Psalms 23:6)

— **KEY VERSE** —

What do you think? If a man has a hundred sheep, and one of them has gone astray, does he not leave the ninety-nine on the mountains and go in search of the one that went astray? (Matthew 18:12)

GOD TIME

READ : Matthew 18:10-14
WRITE : Matthew 18:12

....

....

REFLECT :
- How might 1 Timothy 4:12 relate to today's passage, and how can you apply it to your life?
- Read 1 Thessalonians 5:11. How do you build up the body of Christ?
- Read John 10: 11-16. What further insights does this passage add to today's parable?
- Memorize Ephesians 4:32.
- Make a list of the ways you know you bring joy to God.

RESPOND :

....

....

....

....

....

PLAN TIME

THINGS TO DO (3-5 MAX) :

KEY EVENTS TODAY :

MOVE TIME

MORNING WATER ☐

B : _____
L : _____
D : _____

SNACK :

SIMPLE WORKOUT ☐

WEEK 4, DAY 4: LUKE 15:11-19

NOTING TODAY'S SETTING OF LUKE 15 IS IMPORTANT. The Gospel writer, Luke, shares that in the crowd listening to Jesus are tax collectors and sinners. Keeping a close eye on the Law and lawbreakers, the Pharisees were disgruntled that Jesus spent time with vile tax collectors and broke bread with sinners. (Luke 15:1-2) The message of this week's parables, seeking and saving the lost, made Pharisees squirm.

The parable of The Prodigal Son begins with sin. A young man, the younger of two brothers, breaks the fifth commandment: *"Honor your father and mother, that your days may be long in the land the Lord your God is giving you."* (Exodus 20:12) Deeply dishonoring his father, he asks for his inheritance early. Even today, inheritances are not distributed until the person giving it has died. The younger son's request is like saying, "Dad, I wish you were dead."

With an inheritance in hand, the prodigal (meaning "wasteful") son departs for *"a far country, and there he squandered his property in reckless living."* So much sin is done in the dark, in hiding, or in a location where sin is not only tolerated but encouraged. Trading the promise of the fifth commandment for "Sin City," the younger son falls into the cycle of sin. The apostle James writes, *"Then desire when it has conceived gives birth to sin, and sin when it is fully grown brings forth death."* (James 1:15) The downward spiral continues until the prodigal "hits rock-bottom."

Reaching the end of himself and his money in a land that is as destitute as he, the Bible says, *"he came to himself."* (Luke 15:17) An epiphany in a pig pen! No matter how far away he traveled, the young man can't escape the memories of his loving and patient father. He takes responsibility for his bad behavior and repents, turns back from his dead-end living to return to the father who loves him so much.

As a disciple of Jesus, I am reminded to protect and honor my relationships. As a mother and a discipler of daughters, I am instructed to give them freedom to establish their own relationship with God and trust Him for the results. Following Jesus, I heed the warning that if I am hiding my behavior, it is probably sinful. Last, but not least, there is no dead-end that I can't turn back from because God always makes a way.

— **KEY VERSE** —

I will arise and go to my father, and I will say to him, "Father, I have sinned against heaven and before you." (Luke 15:18)

Hello mornings
God. Plan. Move.

GOD TIME

READ : Luke 15:11-19
WRITE : Luke 15:18

. . . .

. . . .

. . . .

REFLECT :
- Chart the who, what, when, why, where, and how of this passage.
- Contrast the command and promise in Exodus 20:12 with the actions and consequences of the prodigal son.
- Research the cultural context of this parable. What did you learn?
- Outline the passage.
- Read Colossians 1:13-14; what is your response to this passage and today's parable?

RESPOND :

. . . .

. . . .

. . . .

. . . .

. . . .

PLAN TIME

THINGS TO DO (3-5 MAX) :

KEY EVENTS TODAY :

MOVE TIME

MORNING WATER ☐

B : _____
L : _____
D : _____

SNACK :

SIMPLE WORKOUT ☐

AS THE STORY OF THE PRODIGAL SON COMES TO COMPLETION, we see the God who is a friend of sinners, who forgives our deepest sins, and who is quick to lavish the bounty of His grace on those who turn to Him. As a disciple of Jesus, this is the God I want the world to know.

While the prodigal son was still far off, the father *"saw him and felt compassion, and ran and embraced him and kissed him."* (Luke 15:20) Jewish fathers never ran to their children; children ran to their fathers. All propriety cast aside, the running father is indeed indicative of God's character: the God who searches the whole house for one coin, the God who leaves ninety-nine faithful ones to find the one who is lost is the God who runs to meet the repentant sinner.

As soon as the father greets his prodigal son, confession of sin and request for forgiveness burst forth. (Luke 15:21) Confession is part of God's plan: *"If we confess our sins, he is faithful and just to forgive us our sins and to cleanse us from all unrighteousness."* (1 John 1:9) I can confess my sins freely because God assures my forgiveness and restoration. As a disciple of Jesus, the Holy Spirit desires confession to continue the discipleship process. Confession helps clear out the muck of sin, so I can continue to give up everything that keeps me from being closer to Jesus.

An act of grace, the father orders an extravagant feast. A robe, a ring, and shoes- all signs of a son in good standing- the father pours out his blessings on his son who has returned. Likewise, God lavishly gives *"spiritual blessings,"* sparing no expense. Among these are forgiveness, grace, and redemption. (Ephesians 1:2-10)

Meanwhile, the son who stayed is affronted by his father's actions toward his younger brother. Just as he ran to his younger son, the gracious father pursues his older son. (Luke 25:28) After the older son's rude rant, the father says, *"'Son, you are always with me, and all that is mine is yours.'"* As a disciple of Jesus, I want to root out judgmental attitudes and welcome all whom God restores.

This story of the prodigal son gives me confidence, encouragement, and hope as I continue my journey of discipleship. Even if I get lost along the way, I know that "nothing is lost that can't be found."

— **KEY VERSE** —

It was fitting to celebrate and be glad, for this your brother was dead, and is alive; he was lost, and is found. (Luke 15:32)

Hello mornings
God. Plan. Move.

READ : Luke 15:20-32
WRITE : Luke 15:32

. . . .

. . . .

REFLECT :
- Illustrate today's passage. (word art, sketch the story, etc.)
- Consider listening to the song "When God Ran." Here is a link to a version by Phillips, Craig and Dean: *https://youtu.be/Tx97Jrbrhvw* Can you picture God running to you?
- What difference does it make in your life that God runs to you?
- Read 1 John 1:9, and spend time in prayer confessing your sin.
- Read a commentary concerning this passage. What new insight did you gain?

RESPOND :

. . . .

. . . .

. . . .

. . . .

. . . .

PLAN TIME

THINGS TO DO (3-5 MAX) :

KEY EVENTS TODAY :

MOVE TIME

MORNING WATER ☐

B : _____

L : _____

D : _____

SNACK :

SIMPLE WORKOUT ☐

WEEK FIVE

by Patti Brown

WEEK 5, DAY 1: LUKE 16:1-13

BRITISH PREACHER AND FOUNDER OF METHODISM JOHN WESLEY grew up in extreme poverty in the early 1700's, but achieved success as a university professor and became financially well-off. The story is told that one cold day, after purchasing some pictures to hang in his room, he noticed a chambermaid with no coat. When he went to give her some money he discovered he had little left to give. Stricken, he determined to limit his expenses so he would have more money to give to the poor. As his income increased, he did not increase his expenses. He did so for the remainder of his life. It is said that one year he gave away 98% of his income!

Our first parable this week is one of the most debated parables in the New Testament. But all agree that money plays a significant role. It may help you understand the parable better if you realize that Jesus did not present the steward as a man to emulate. The steward was not faithful with the money he was given. But Jesus recognized that believers would have to manage money, and He wanted to guide them.

Money is always a challenge to handle wisely, because it is so easy to turn into an idol. This is why Jesus said *"it is easier for a camel to go through the eye of a needle than for a rich person to enter the kingdom of God."* (Matthew 19:24) Money enslaves, and wealth will ultimately fail you if you put your hope in it. But money can provide for others' needs. You can be *"wise as serpents and innocent as doves"* (Matthew 10:16) with that which is of the world and use it to love and serve the needy.

"Whatever we have, the property of it is God's; we have only the use of it, according to the direction of our great Lord, and for his honour. This steward wasted his lord's goods. And we are all liable to the same charge; we have not made due improvement of what God has trusted us with." —Matthew Henry

Jesus draws a clear line in the sand: you simply can't love money and love God. You have to choose. And when you choose God, you can use the money He gives you to serve others and bring Him glory.

Lord help me to always choose you. Amen.

— **KEY VERSE** —

No servant can serve two masters, for either he will hate the one and love the other, or he will be devoted to the one and despise the other. You cannot serve God and money. (Luke 16:13)

Hello mornings
God. Plan. Move.

READ : Luke 16:1-13
WRITE : Luke 16:13

....

....

REFLECT :
- Is there anything that challenges you in this passage? Write down your questions.
- Read other perspectives on this parable: *https://carm.org/parable-unjust-steward* or *https://goo.gl/2FCQeS*.
- What does Scripture say about money in Ecclesiastes 5:10, 1 Timothy 6:10, and Hebrews 13:5?
- Does the way you handle money align with God's Word?
- What small things has God asked you to be faithful with in this season? (See Luke 16:10.)

RESPOND :

....

....

....

....

....

PLAN TIME

THINGS TO DO (3-5 MAX) :

MOVE TIME

MORNING WATER ☐

B : _____

L : _____

D : _____

KEY EVENTS TODAY :

SNACK :

SIMPLE WORKOUT ☐

THE FRONT WALKWAY TO MY HOUSE IS CONCRETE, but it is often covered with little shards of rock. Not in a decorative way—unless you have a ten-year-old's sense of style. You see, the ten-year-old who lives in my house is a rock hunter. He prowls around our property gathering ugly rocks and smashing them with a hammer on the front walkway, hoping to reveal a treasure inside. His efforts are not in vain. Happily for him we live in an area with plentiful geodes.

The rich man in today's parable was interested in treasure too, but not the hidden kind. His was a world of extravagance—expensive clothes and feasting were his norm. He couldn't be bothered with a sick, starving man who was so unwell that others had to carry him to his gates to beg for scraps.

The rich man had everything he needed to be comfortable while he was alive. But his comforts distracted him from eternity, even though he had full access to Scriptures— "Moses and the Prophets"—that would have kept his focus in the right place. You and I dare not be too judgmental of him. Our comforts can be distracting as well.

"The riches of this world are deceitful and uncertain. Let us be convinced that those are truly rich, and very rich, who are rich in faith, and rich toward God, rich in Christ, in the promises; let us then lay up our treasure in heaven, and expect our portion from thence." —Matthew Henry

The rich man wanted Lazarus to rise from the dead to warn his brothers, but Abraham's message was clear: If you don't believe the Word, there isn't much that will convince you. Paul wrote that *"All Scripture is breathed out by God and profitable for teaching, for reproof, for correction, and for training in righteousness, that the man of God may be complete, equipped for every good work."* (2 Timothy 3:16-17) And just prior to today's passage, Jesus said in Luke 16:17, *"It is easier for heaven and earth to pass away than for one stroke of a letter of the Law to fail."* The Word of God is trustworthy and true!

All you need to know about life on earth and in heaven is wrapped up in the Bible on your lap. Like a humble rock that contains a beautiful geode, that unassuming Book contains true treasure.

Lord, bind my heart to you and to your Word. Amen.

— **KEY VERSE** —

But Abraham said, 'They have Moses and the Prophets; let them hear them.' (Luke 16:29)

Hello mornings
God. Plan. Move.

READ : Luke 16:19-31
WRITE : Luke 16:29

....

....

REFLECT :
- – How does today's parable continue the message of the parable we studied yesterday?
- – Read 2 Timothy 3:16 and 2 Peter 1:21. Who is the source of Scripture?
- – How does the Holy Spirit help us with the Word? (See John 14:26, John 16:8, and 1 Corinthians 2:12.)
- – What is the treasure and its vessel in 2 Corinthians 4:5-7?
- – The rich man missed his opportunity to serve Lazarus. Ask God to show you whom He would like you to serve today.

RESPOND :

....

....

....

....

PLAN TIME

THINGS TO DO (3-5 MAX) :

KEY EVENTS TODAY :

MOVE TIME

MORNING WATER ☐

B : _____
L : _____
D : _____

SNACK :

SIMPLE WORKOUT ☐

WEEK 5, DAY 3: MATTHEW 20:1-16

A LEGEND IS TOLD OF TSARINA MARIA FYODOROVNA, wife to Tsar Alexander II of Russia, that she once saved a prisoner by means of a comma. The warrant for his imprisonment and death read "Pardon impossible, send to Siberia." Maria transposed the comma on the warrant, changing the message to "Pardon, impossible to send to Siberia," thus saving his life. Just as the prisoner did not deserve that punctuation rearrangement, the eleventh hour laborers in today's parable did not deserve a full denarius. But grace does not employ the word "deserve."

In his final hours, the thief on the cross—a rightfully convicted criminal—accepted Jesus and was welcomed into eternity (Luke 23:39-43). Up until their final breath, every single person has the opportunity to turn to the Lord and repent. Grace and forgiveness are equally offered to all. As the master says: *"Am I not allowed to do what I choose with what belongs to me? Or do you begrudge my generosity?"* (Matthew 20:15)

But for some reason we want things to be "fair" don't we? Like the laborers who worked for twelve hours and resented the master's payment to the final workers, we wonder how someone who has done wrong his whole life can be forgiven. Woe to us if that notion of "fair" was what God used! Fair would mean we got what we deserved, too. Instead we should rejoice that *"He does not deal with us according to our sins, nor repay us according to our iniquities."* (Psalm 103:10)

"We are accustomed to finding a catch in every promise, but Jesus' stories of extravagant grace include no catch, no loophole disqualifying us from God's love." —Philip Yancey

There is nothing in all creation that can separate us from the love of God in Christ Jesus (Romans 8:38-39). He graciously holds out the offer of His love, and eternity with Him, to each and every human on earth, no matter their past. God is constantly moving commas. His grace is limitless and His generosity incomprehensible.

Lord, thank you for your limitless grace. Amen.

— KEY VERSE —

Am I not allowed to do what I choose with what belongs to me? Or do you begrudge my generosity? (Matthew 20:15)

GOD TIME

READ : Matthew 20:1-16
WRITE : Matthew 20:15

....

....

REFLECT :
 – Write a timeline of the events in today's parable.
 – What do you think Matthew 20:16 means? Give examples from your life.
 – What does Luke 23:39-43 tell you about grace?
 – Read Romans 8:38-39. List the things that cannot come between you and the love of Christ.
 – Write a prayer of thanksgiving to God for His generous grace to you.

RESPOND :

....

....

....

....

....

PLAN TIME

THINGS TO DO (3-5 MAX) :

KEY EVENTS TODAY :

MOVE TIME

MORNING WATER ☐

B : _____
L : _____
D : _____

SNACK :

SIMPLE WORKOUT ☐

WEEK 5, DAY 4: LUKE 18:1-8

OUR FAMILY IS BLESSED TO LIVE IN THE TEXAS COUNTRYSIDE. The summer after purchasing some new acreage, my husband came back from a walk bursting with news: "There is a huge blackberry patch downstream of the pond!" My first blackberry expedition was successful; I came back with buckets of fruit, and scratches all over my arms and legs. First lesson: wear a long sleeved- shirt and pants. I rinsed the bugs and leaves off the berries and set a big bowl of them on the table. We sat down to enjoy the berries and our mouths puckered up. Second lesson: learn how to identify fully ripened blackberries.

What does today's parable have to do with blackberries? Those not-quite-ripe blackberries remind me of something I think we all have: unanswered prayers. Or at least that's how we view them. This parable reminds us that unanswered prayers are simply prayers that are not answered yet. Once again, Jesus uses a worldly situation with unrighteous people to explain a heavenly truth: perseverance in making requests to God bears fruit.

Why doesn't God just answer our prayers right away? While we can't know the mind of God, we can see how a delayed response might be a blessing. Often God is working on things that we cannot see, details that we don't even realize have bearing on our situation. Sometimes God is working on *us*, growing our patience and faith, healing broken parts of our hearts that need to be made whole before we can receive His answer to our prayer.

Occasionally we may not even realize that He has already answered us. This could be because we are not spiritually mature enough to recognize His answer, or because He has simply said no. If something we request is not in His will, we know He will not grant it.

"In the old days of flint, steel, and brimstone matches, people had to strike the match again and again, perhaps even dozens of times, before they could get a spark to light their fire, and they were very thankful if they finally succeeded. Should we not have the same kind of perseverance and hope regarding heavenly things?" —Charles Spurgeon

Jesus asks at the end of this passage: will the Son of Man find faith on earth? Just as the widow faithfully presented her petitions to the judge, we must faithfully and patiently present our requests to God. Our faith in Him is the solid ground upon which we pray without ceasing.

Lord, help me to persevere in prayer and patiently wait for your perfect timing. Amen.

—  KEY VERSE —

And he told them a parable to the effect that they ought always to pray and not lose heart. (Luke 18:1)

Hello mornings
God. Plan. Move.

READ : Luke 18:1-8
WRITE : Luke 18:1

. . . .

. . . .

REFLECT :
- Write out Romans 12:12 in your journal.
- What does 1 Thessalonians 5:17 look like in your life?
- What do these verses tell you about prayer: 1 John 5:14-15, Matthew 21:22, Proverbs 15:29, Psalm 66:17-20.
- Re-read today's key verse, then read 2 Corinthians 4:16-18. Why can we not lose heart?
- Is there anything you have given up praying about? Spend time in conversation with God.

RESPOND :

. . . .

. . . .

. . . .

. . . .

. . . .

PLAN TIME

THINGS TO DO (3-5 MAX) :

KEY EVENTS TODAY :

MOVE TIME

MORNING WATER ☐

B : _____

L : _____

D : _____

SNACK :

SIMPLE WORKOUT ☐

WEEK 5, DAY 5: LUKE 18:9-14

IF I HAD TO PICK THE JOB I'D LEAST LIKE TO DO, pumping septic tanks would probably be near the top of the list. Larry Goodwill did not share my opinion. For Larry (and yes, Goodwill was his real last name) pumping tanks meant the opportunity to meet and talk with people all over our county. Larry was on fire for Jesus and used the humblest of jobs as a means to share the Gospel. One of his favorite things to say to his customers was "You never know when you will take your last breath, so get right with Jesus!" Several years ago Larry was killed when a UPS truck hit his septic truck head on. He went straight from his mission field into the arms of his Savior.

Luke tells us that Jesus specifically directed today's parable to contemptuous people who trusted in their own righteousness. Do you ever do that? Trust in yourself? Something in our nature makes us want to have a "Christian to-do list." Tithing? Check. Fasting? Check. Volunteer at church? Check. If you check off the whole list, you'll know you are a good Christian, right?

Wrong. God cares about what you do, yes. But what you do should come from the overflow of a heart beating in time with Jesus' heart, not a desire to look good to others. In the Jewish culture of Jesus' time, a Pharisee was believed to be a good and upright member of society, while a tax collector was despised and considered a swindler. Yet Jesus saw right into their hearts. The Pharisee's heart was hardened and prideful. But the tax collector's heart was soft and humble, able to be shaped to be more like the Lord's.

In God's economy, what is most valuable is not how you appear on the outside, but whose you are on the inside. Pride takes your focus off God and puts it on yourself. C.S. Lewis wrote, *"Pride leads to every other vice: it is the complete anti-God state of mind."* When we humbly put God and others first, we are in right relationship with the world. *"Do nothing from selfish ambition or conceit, but in humility count others more significant than yourselves."* Philippians 2:3

After Larry Goodwill died, a woman who was a single mother told how Larry's humility had impacted her life. He had fixed a serious septic issue for her for $2000 less than anyone else would and shared the Gospel with her that day. He had invited her to church—she attended the very next Sunday. Dwight L. Moody said, *"Of one hundred men, one will read the Bible; the ninety-nine will read the Christian."* I want to be a book that tells all about Jesus, don't you?

Lord, may there be less of me and more of you each day. Amen.

—  KEY VERSE —

For everyone who exalts himself will be humbled, but the one who humbles himself will be exalted. (Luke 18:14b)

GOD TIME

READ : Luke 18:9-14
WRITE : Luke 18:14b

. . . .

. . . .

REFLECT :
  – Read Matthew 6:1-6. What are the two types of rewards?
  – List the reasons Jesus condemns the Pharisees in Matthew 23:25-28.
  – Research the beliefs of Pharisees and the role of tax collectors in Jesus' time.
  – Jonathan Edwards said, "We must view humility as one of the most essential things that characterizes true Christianity." Do you agree or disagree? Why?
  – Write out Philippians 2:3-8. Ask God to show you areas where you need to grow.

RESPOND :

. . . .

. . . .

. . . .

. . . .

. . . .

PLAN TIME

THINGS TO DO (3-5 MAX) :

KEY EVENTS TODAY :

MOVE TIME

MORNING WATER ☐

B : _____

L : _____

D : _____

SNACK :

SIMPLE WORKOUT ☐

WEEK SIX

by Kelli LaFram

WEEK 6, DAY 1: LUKE: 19:12-26

I HAVE FOUR CHILDREN AND THEY ARE ALL EXPECTED to help with the household chores. I am able to clean and care for the home on my own. And goodness! Some days training my children to do the dishes or the laundry is more work than just doing it myself. But I keep at it, hoping the effort will lead to four positive and productive members of society.

In today's passage, we also see some positive and productive individuals and some who are not so much.

The nobleman represents Jesus, the servants represent believers in Christ, and the citizens represent the rest of mankind who refuse to submit to Jesus's authority. The minas? They represent the Gospel, which each believer is given in equal measure just as the nobleman gave minas in equal measure to his servants.

Before the nobleman left to receive his kingdom, he gave each of his servants a mina and instructed them to "do business till I come" (Luke 19:13, NKJV)

Jesus gave each of us the same instructions, as well: *All authority in heaven and on earth has been given to me. Go therefore and make disciples of all nations, baptizing them in the name of the Father and of the Son and of the Holy Spirit, teaching them to observe all that I have commanded you. And behold, I am with you always, to the end of the age.* (Matthew 28:18-20)

We servants are to "do business" with the Gospel. That business? Make disciples. Jesus doesn't need us for this work. He is able to do it on His own, just as I am able to do the household chores on my own. He knows that we will make mistakes as we share the Gospel, just as my children will make mistakes with the dishes and the laundry. Yet Jesus invites us into the work anyway, teaching and refining us through the process.

We have two options when we hear the invitation to do business: We can gladly take His mina, allow the Holy Spirit to work through us, and watch His kingdom grow. Or we can take the mina, hide it away, and make excuses for our inaction. The choice is ours.

— **KEY VERSE** —

So he called ten of his servants, delivered to them ten minas, and said to them, 'Do business till I come.' (Luke 19:13, NKJV)

Hello mornings

God. Plan. Move.

READ : Luke 19:12-26
WRITE : Luke 19:13

. . . .

. . . .

REFLECT :
- Folding your paper in half lengthwise, creating two columns. Write the entire passage on the left side. On the right jot down any ideas, questions, or verses that come to mind.
- Read the key verse in multiple translations. Meditate on what it means to "do business."
- Pray, asking God to reveal to you the next step of doing business for Him.
- Illustrate a picture of yourself doing business for God's kingdom.
- Read verses 25-26. What is your initial reaction? Does it line up with Jesus's teaching?

RESPOND :

. . . .

. . . .

. . . .

. . . .

PLAN TIME

THINGS TO DO (3-5 MAX) :

MOVE TIME

MORNING WATER ☐

B : _____

L : _____

D : _____

KEY EVENTS TODAY :

SNACK :

SIMPLE WORKOUT ☐

WEEK 6, DAY 2: MATTHEW 21:28-32

YESTERDAY WE READ ABOUT TWO TYPES OF SERVANTS. One willing to "do business" with the Gospel for Jesus and one willing to sit idle with the good news. Today we see two sons. The first rejects the instructions of his father, but then decides to get on board. The other tells the father what he thinks the father wants to hear but does the opposite.

The questions that Jesus asked had an obvious answer. *"Which of the two did the will of his father?"* The first, of course. But what may not be so obvious is the answer to this question: which son am I more like? Ask yourself that. Which son best represents you?

A few years ago I wouldn't have wanted to honestly answer this question. Sure, I knew what the Great Commission was. I knew (or thought I knew) the importance of making disciples. But I wasn't really doing the business that my Savior had called me to do.

I wasn't intentionally spending time with people who needed to know Jesus. I wasn't intentionally teaching my children about Him. Well, I was, but so they could give the correct Sunday School answer and I could pat myself on the back. I wasn't teaching them so they would hunger for their own relationship with Christ.

I was a woman who showed up to church. I said the pretty prayers. I did my Bible study. Occasionally, I even said, "Lord, send me." But then nothing. No action. No follow through. I said and did what I thought my Father wanted to hear, but like the second son in the parable, I did not go.

Praise the Lord, however, the Spirit got ahold of me and taught me the way of righteousness. The way John came preaching of (Matthew 21:32). It is further explained in 1 John 1:9:

If we confess our sins, he is faithful and just to forgive us our sins and to cleanse us from all unrighteousness.

Friends, take a slow and carefully look at your life and those in it. Are you making disciples as you have been instructed? If the answer is yes, awesome! Keep at it. But if the answer is no, it is time to simply repent, rejoice in God's forgiveness and His cleansing power. Then be about "doing business" till He comes.

— KEY VERSE —

If we confess our sins, he is faithful and just to forgive us our sins and to cleanse us from all unrighteousness. (1 John 1:9)

Hello mornings
God. Plan. Move.

READ : Matthew 21:28-32
WRITE : 1 John 1:9

....

....

REFLECT :
- Folding your paper in half lengthwise, creating two columns. Write the entire passage on the left side. On the right jot down any ideas, questions, or verses that come to mind.
- Read verse 29. How is this son righteous? (Hint: read the key verse)
- In 1 John 1:9, God promises to forgive and cleanse us. What is this promise contingent on?
- Does this passage lead me to confess anything in prayer?
- Memorize the key verse this week.

RESPOND :

....

....

....

....

....

....

PLAN TIME

THINGS TO DO (3-5 MAX) :

KEY EVENTS TODAY :

MOVE TIME

MORNING WATER ☐

B : _____

L : _____

D : _____

SNACK :

SIMPLE WORKOUT ☐

WEEK 6, DAY 3: MATTHEW 21:33-46

"HAVE YOU NEVER READ THE SCRIPTURES...?" Jesus asked. Can you imagine the offense the chief priests and Pharisees took to this question. Have we ever read the Scriptures? Who does He think we are? Can you see their eyes roll? Can you hear the disgust in their voice?

Of course, they had read the Scriptures, but it was clear that they did not understand them. All of Scripture had pointed to Jesus and here He was, standing before them and yet they didn't believe.

These men, the descendants of Aaron, were the priests assigned to do the business of pointing others to the coming Messiah. They were to act justly and live righteously. Many did, I'm sure, yet most oppressed the people and refused to teach them of their Savior (Isaiah 5:7). They neglected God's business and promoted themselves time and again, going through all the religious activities in order to be seen, admired, and to inherit a reward they wrongly believed they were owed.

Yes, they had read, but they didn't understand. And so, as Jesus warned, the kingdom of God was taken from them and given to another nation bearing the fruit of it. A nation built on the Chief Cornerstone, indwelt by the Holy Spirit, taught by the apostles, and sent forth to make disciples of all nations. This nation? Us. Christ's Church.

We are the nation that God intends to bear the fruit of His kingdom. Sweet, good fruit that points others to Jesus. Fruit produced when we faithfully spend time in God's Word for the sake of being with Him. Fruit that is offered in praise and thanksgiving. Fruit that begins to grow when we choose to come down from our high places and fall face-down in worship on the Chief Cornerstone. Kingdom fruit only happens when we allow Jesus to sweetly break us of pride, arrogance, and entitlement. We become fruit-bearers when we humbly surrender our lives to Him.

I don't know about you, but I can be just like the men who plotted to take my Savior's— their Savior's—life. I often do business that draws attention to myself and forget all about the One who sees me fully and loves me anyway. Oh, how I need grace! I am so thankful for the simple way of righteousness (1 John 1:9), aren't you?

— KEY VERSE —

And the one who falls on this stone will be broken to pieces; and when it falls on anyone, it will crush him. (Matthew 21:44)

Hello mornings
God. Plan. Move.

READ : Matthew 21:33-46
WRITE : Matthew 21:44

. . . .

. . . .

. . . .

REFLECT :
- Folding your paper in half lengthwise, creating two columns. Write the entire passage on the left side. On the right jot down any ideas, questions, or verses that come to mind.
- Continue memorizing yesterday's key verse.
- Study the original Greek word for "falls" in the key verse.
- Read Isaiah 5:1-7. How does this compare to today's passage?
- Does this passage lead me to confess anything in prayer?

RESPOND :

. . . .

. . . .

. . . .

. . . .

. . . .

PLAN TIME

THINGS TO DO (3-5 MAX) :

KEY EVENTS TODAY :

MOVE TIME

MORNING WATER ☐

B : _____

L : _____

D : _____

SNACK :

SIMPLE WORKOUT ☐

WEEK 6, DAY 4: MATTHEW 22:1-14

WHAT A PARABLE! A king invites many to a feast that he has prepared. He relentlessly sends his servants out — not once, but twice — with the invitation. Yet his subjects refuse the offer. Some even beat and kill the king's servants. Unbelievable.

The king, of course, does not let these cruel people go unpunished and destroys their lives and homes.

Next, he sends his servants out again to invite others to the feast. Others—both bad and good—as many as his servants can find. And they come. They come in such great number that the banquet hall is full beyond belief. Then the king sees a man without a wedding garment and asks, *"Friend, how did you come in here without a wedding garment?"* The man refuses to answer and the king has him bound and cast into outer darkness.

Do these last few verses leave you a little confused? Are you wondering, *Wait! Is it the man's fault that he does not have a wedding garment?* Well, actually it is, because just as we are offered clothes of righteousness when we accept the invitation of salvation (Isaiah 61:10, Revelation 19:8), the man too was offered a wedding garment when he accepted the invitation to the banquet. He did not take the garment however, and he could not give the king a reason for his actions. Friend the king had called him, as in, "dear fellow, it's not too late." But the man remained silent, refusing the king's gift of beautiful adornment. Amazing.

Do you know who else amazes me, but in a good way? The king's servants. They repeatedly went out with the invitation, even after their fellow laborers had been beaten and killed. Simply amazing! They must have loved their master. They must have been fully committed to him and to doing his business. Do you see where I'm going with this?

Because of love, we too need to be committed to our King and to doing His business. We are to go out time and again with the message of the Gospel. We are to gather all who will come and make disciples of them.

Not because we are trying to earn clothes of righteousness, but because we have already been dressed in them. Not because we are pursuing favor or love, but because we are already loved and favored by a King who first relentlessly pursued us.

— **KEY VERSE** —

Go therefore to the main roads and invite to the wedding feast as many as you find. (Matthew 22:9)

Hello mornings
God. Plan. Move.

READ : Matthew 22:1-14
WRITE : Matthew 22:9

....

....

REFLECT :
- Folding your paper in half lengthwise, creating two columns. Write the entire passage on the left side. On the right jot down any ideas, questions, or verses that come to mind.
- Read one or more commentaries from a trusted author on this passage.
- Write a brief summary of the lessons you have taken away from this parable.
- Who can you share the Gospel with today? What might happen if you do?
- Spend some time in prayer. Ask God to show you the next step to take in making disciples.

RESPOND :

....

....

....

....

....

....

PLAN TIME

THINGS TO DO (3-5 MAX) :

KEY EVENTS TODAY :

MOVE TIME

MORNING WATER ☐

B : _____

L : _____

D : _____

SNACK :

SIMPLE WORKOUT ☐

WEEK 6, DAY 5: MATTHEW 25:31-46

Co-written by Kelli LaFram, Kat Lee, and Ali Shaw

I STILL REMEMBER THE STINKY SMELL OF THE MUSTY OLD COTTAGE and the mounds of donated clothing. Though I didn't like the creaky, dank building and didn't want to be there that day, I had volunteered to sort donations at our church's clothes closet where we sold (and sometimes gave) items for next to nothing to those in need. As I buttoned up a men's work shirt with a bad attitude, the words "as you did it to one of the least of these my brothers, you did it to me" popped into my mind. In one second flat, God shifted my perspective and I remembered that His heart is for his people to be loved and cared for.

Jesus said, "Truly, I say to you, as you did it to one of the least of these my brothers, you did it to me." (v. 40, emphasis added). 1 John 3:16-17 says, "By this we know love, that he laid down his life for us, and we ought to lay down our lives for the brothers. But if anyone has the world's goods and sees his brother in need, yet closes his heart against him, how does God's love abide in him?"

It's easy to get distracted by everything in our lives and walk right by those in need all around us. That's why these verses can feel so convicting. Seeing the need can feel overwhelming and paralyzing.

But as Believers, we know we've got the Holy Spirit living inside us and bearing His fruit. It's never too late to begin to notice and open our hearts to God's leading. By His power we are able to love and care for our brothers and sisters.

Let's take time right now to turn to God. If we haven't been loving we need to be honest with Him. He already knows. We only need to confess our sin and He will be faithful and just to forgive and cleanse us of unrighteousness. (1 John 1:9).

We all have it in our hearts to love and serve mankind, but it takes conscious effort coupled with power of the Holy Spirit to step off the merry-go-round of our comfort zones. Though it may inconvenience us, make us uncomfortable at times, and stretch us outside of the routine, God's heart is for His people to be loved and cared for.

Teach us, Lord, to trust the Father, abide in Jesus, rely on the Holy Spirit, and love those You bring into our lives.

— KEY VERSE —

And the King will answer them, 'Truly, I say to you, as you did it to one of the least of these my brothers, you did it to me.' (Matthew 25:40)

Hello mornings
God. Plan. Move.

GOD TIME

READ : Matthew 25:31-36
WRITE : Matthew 25:40

. . . .

. . . .

REFLECT :
- Folding your paper in half lengthwise, creating two columns. Write the entire passage on the left side. On the right jot down any ideas, questions, or verses that come to mind.
- Read 1 John 3:10-23. How are we to act toward our brothers and sisters in Christ?
- Are today's passages leading you to confess anything in prayer?
- Recite aloud 1 John 1:9 several times.
- Spend some time in prayer. Ask God to show you the next step to take in making disciples

RESPOND :

. . . .

. . . .

. . . .

. . . .

PLAN TIME

THINGS TO DO (3-5 MAX) :

KEY EVENTS TODAY :

MOVE TIME

MORNING WATER ☐

B : _____

L : _____

D : _____

SNACK :

SIMPLE WORKOUT ☐

CONCLUSION

I PRAY THAT THIS SIX-WEEK LONG INVITATION to sit quietly with Jesus and listen to His parables has blessed you richly. It's powerful, isn't it? Savoring our Savior's words is truly heart-touching and life-changing. It's because His words are words of life!

When the world around us prizes distractions from the spiritual, we know better. We know the power in being still and listening to the One who cares for us beyond comprehension. It's because of His great love for us that His parables address so many of our hearts struggles. He will never leave us nor forsake us (Deuteronomy 31:6) so He has left His perfect words and His Holy Spirit to guide us.

I pray that this study has dealt with your heart in whatever way God meant for it to. He knows you and knows your every need and care. Because of His great love for us, and His intimate knowledge of how we best learn, His stories equip us to know and live out truth.

Journey on, dear sister, walking in His truth. Carry with you the lessons you've learned from our Savior and the sweetness of His life-giving message. Walk with eternity in mind.

In Him,

Ali

ABOUT THE AUTHORS

ALI SHAW, wife of 20 plus years and mom to three daughters, leads a full, grace-filled life. She is owner of and writer at Do Not Depart *(donotdepart.com)* and also serves on the HelloMornings Leadership team...and is just generally in awe that God will use a regular girl like her!

Woven with practical insight, her writing lovingly encourages women to seek God daily through the reading and study of His Word. She blogs occasionally at Heartfelt Reflections *(heartfeltreflections.wordpress.com)*, where she's written an online Bible study titled Learning from Job *(heartfeltreflections.wordpress.com/2014/01/17/learning-from-job)*. She has also authored an in-depth Bible study of Abigail available as a PDF. For information or encouragement, you can connect with her on Facebook *(www.facebook.com/heartfeltreflectionsblog)*.

ALYSSA J. HOWARD is a wife and stay-at-home mom to two young girls. She lives with her family in the Pacific Northwest where she loves to bake, run, drink coffee, and play with her little ones. Alyssa first fell in love with writing while earning her Master of Arts degree in theological studies through Liberty Theological Seminary, and she has been writing about Jesus and the Christian life for the past two years at *alyssajhoward.com*.

CHELI SIGLER is a home educator, home school co-op administrator, HelloMornings Group Leader, and HelloMornings Group Leader Encourager and Mentor. These are just some of the ways she pursues her God-given purpose. Her husband says, "Cheli needs to teach like a fish needs water." She occasionally appears as a "Word Writer" at Deeper Waters *(deeperwaters.us/day-20-philippians)*, sporadically blogs at Painting Rainbows *(chelisigler.wordpress.com)*, and you can find her on Twitter

as @CheliSigler and Instagram as @chelidee. Cheli lives with her husband and two teenage daughters in Orlando, FL.

KELLI LAFRAM Wife. Mom. Coffee drinker. Bible reader. Jesus believer. Plus a writer, painter, sign-maker, & furniture-flipper. That's Kelli in a nutshell. Kelli has authored And When You Pray: Understanding the Lord's Prayer (*gumroad.com/l/WpNZ*) and Caught by Jesus: a 6-Week Study in the Gospel of Mark (*gumroad.com/l/GJTv*). You can find her letting her light shine at *KelliLaFram.com*, where she shares about all sorts of things—from painting to parenting to prayer—and how they all point back to His goodness, His grace, and His glory.

LINDSEY BELL is the author of the new Bible study and devotional, *Unbeaten (www.lindseymbell.com/books/unbeaten)*, and of the parenting devotional, *Searching for Sanity (amazon.com/dp/1938499751)*. She's a stay-at-home mother of two silly boys, a minister's wife, an avid reader, and a lover of all things chocolate. Lindsey writes weekly at *lindseymbell.com* about faith, family, and learning to love the life she's been given.

PATTI BROWN is a wife, mama to three, and, most importantly, God's girl. She and her family live in rural Texas where they make lots of messes while they sing, write, act, knit, and invent new recipes. In the rare moments when she is not homeschooling or cleaning up messes, she is a women's ministry leader and a writer. You can find her writing with a team of authors at Do Not Depart (*donotdepart.com*), on her blog at Joyful Mama (*joyfulmama.com*), and with her daughter at Blossoms and Posies (*blossomsandposies.com*). Patti joined her first HelloMornings challenge in November of 2010 and was blessed to work in leadership with HelloMornings for three years.

71106176R00043

Made in the USA
Columbia, SC
20 May 2017